GRANT JONES

Voices
of
Coyote Springs Farm

A CHORUS FROM THE MOUTH OF THE CANYON

Skookumchuck Press
Pioneer Square
Oroville

Voices
of
Coyote Springs Farm

A CHORUS FROM THE MOUTH OF THE CANYON

Dedication:

I dedicate this collection of poems to those who speak for clouds, creeks, canyons, critters, trees, old buildings, and all those people who passed this way before whose souls are listening still.

Acknowledgements:

I wish to give my deepest thanks to my old friend and fellow Roethke Advanced Verse Writing classmate, Mike Robinson, Tacoma poet, teacher, newspaper writer and fly fisherman, for his hands-on review of these poems as well as for his crafty mentoring which made many of these poems bloom out of everyday experiences; and to my wife, Chong-hui Chu Jones for her unending support, sustenance, healing and wisdom shared through our wandering paths of living in this unique place that we try to steward and find solace inhabiting.

Publisher's Note:

To my dear friend Walter Henze, co-founder with me of Okanogan Land Trust Poetry Potlucks that we've held the last ten years, and co-editor with me of *OKANOGAN POEMS Volumes 3 Landscapes Are Observatories,* I extend my profound thanks. His design and management skills have also been essential to expediting the printing and distribution of this book as well as the one he helped me publish before, *IN LOVE WITH MY PLACE*, with assistance from the CreateSpace Team at Amazon.

Grant Jones, Publisher
Skookumchuck Press
Pioneer Square
Jones & Jones, Ltd., 105 S. Main Street, Suite 300, Seattle, WA 98104

ISBN: 0-9796495-4-4

Voices
of
Coyote Springs Farm

Introduction

Two poems in this gathering from Grant rise over the others, not because they are better or best. That's a matter of taste.

These two poems simply tell more of his truths. In "**Questions of Healing**" and "**Falling in Love with the Land,**" Grant asks and answers questions about what led him and his wife to turn their backs on Washington's West side to dig into a sunburnt hill North of Omak.

In that first poem, he asks himself, "*What the hell would you be doing if you'd stayed in the city?* He answers that question in all the other poems here.

In the second poem, he delivers the textures that turned this landscape artist into a bare-knuckle farmer who battles broken ground and mounds of poison ivy of an abandoned orchard to transform 50 acres into an arboretum that celebrates the Earth's rejuvenative power.

I have seen most of these poems over the past four years. Seeing them again, what I notice most are the verbs. They crackle like giftwrapping, or like the land underfoot as you walk the trails through the groves he has planted with Chong. It's a good walk.

Mike Robinson
Dash Point

Preface

I live with my wife, Chong, on a farm nestled in the canyon mouth of a long string of foothills which crowd the eastern side of the narrow valley floor of the North Central tributary of the Columbia River called the Okanogan, which in the Interior Salish languages means, "meeting place." Here people of over a dozen of the original tribes still provide leadership to the rest of us who make up this diverse community of Okanogan Country. The foothills where I write form the leading edge of the metamorphosed granitic Okanogan Highlands, a skyward savanna which is the southern finger of the Monashee Range of the Columbia Mountains of British Columbia. A mile to the west across our narrow valley, the limestone faces of the North Cascade Mountains advance inevitably toward us. Like all living things, this landscape has always needed partners, needed caretakers, stewards. It welcomed us when we came over from the San Juan Islands during the summer of 2006 and it sized us up right away. And it continues to give us advice now. In fact over the last twelve years it has quieted us and kept us in one piece.

Grant Jones
Coyote Springs Farm - Jones Riverbraids Nursery Arboretum
Mouth of the Canyon of the Little Mosquito
South Distributary of Mosquito Creek
Sixth downstream tributary of the American Okanogan River
Okanogan Sub Basin of the Columbia River

Grant Jones

Dylan's Cartref, Laugharne 15 June 2002 6pm
Boathouse

"The earth is actually our client, our partner in a life relationship. We need to think about our personal relationships with the land, because the landscape is not a fuzzy, vague or indefinable thing; it's as real as your mother and father and it's everything for you."

Grant Jones

Coyote Springs Farm at the mouth of the Canyon of the Little Mosquito
Looking northwest toward Whiskey Mountain and the confluence of the
Similkameen and Okanogan Rivers below the Oroville-Osoyoos Gap below
the border with Canada, where the North Cascades ssubcontinent meets
the subcontinent of the Okanogan Highlands.

○

This book opens with a couple poem-echoes from the past.

The rest are of this place,
They're voices of right now, of grass, shrub and tree,
Voices of rocks, sand and falling water;
Voices of creatures that swim, ooze, crawl, and slither;
Voices of creatures that walk and leap,
Voices that flutter, flash and soar, and
Voices of builders of sheds, great barns, and old hotels.
Some have already left, but their voices and feelings remain.

Together, they hum in a chorus
That commingles in the rising air,
Making a family of clouds to watch over us,
Whispering stories in the morning mist and afternoon wind.
These are all voices that pry us open and set us straight.
They will also whack us about the head if we're not listening.

Grant Jones   December 25, 2017

ECHOES

Half Through

I've always been
just about through.
When I got my first car at nineteen,
a '57 Chevy,
I blasted through
every stop sign,
with several wrecks under my belt
I didn't think
I'd make it
past twenty-one.

After I turned twenty-three,
l worked for landscape
guru, mentor Haag.
I said "Rich, it's all over.
According to the actuarial charts
I'm half dead."

In 1980
when ASLA*
made me one of its youngest Fellows,
I thought I was living on
borrowed time,
though I started to relax a little
and I made it past forty.

Then, the strangest thing happened
when I turned sixty-one
in the summer of 1999.
It was like starting all over.
I was in Wales with Chong
below the mouth of the Taf,
in Laugharne,
and I realized I had
my whole life ahead of me.

After working for myself or forty years,
I retired at seventy-two
to plant my own arboretum in the Okanogan
at the mouth of the canyon of the Mosquito on fifty
acres of the original Peterson and Stansbury
homesteads quarter-section.
We named our place Coyote Springs Farm
after a string of aspen seeps
up the canyon still yipping out of its dens.
We've become coyotes ourselves.
I guess I'll never be through.

*The American Society of Landscape Architects, founded in 1889. by Frederick Law Olmsted

November 29, 2015
Coyote Springs Farm

Sky-Blue Bosoms

I'm not as pure
As you think you know.
My initiation passage
Happened in Leavenworth
On the Icicle
At fifteen.
I had no idea
The sweet Red
Delicious apples,
Yellow-bellied Ponderosa
Pines and dancing Sockeye salmon
Could braid such warm hearts
To hold me tight.
Those old gentlemen in the road crew
Took me along
That warm, July evening.
Gave me fourth dibs
Those summery sky-blue bosoms.
I have respected elder women
From the country ever since.
Summers continue to bring out
The best in me.

Leavenworth on the Icicle River
Wenatchee Sub Basin
July 1953

"There is no landscape without people; we leave stories and we leave marks and spirits behind imbedded and abiding in the landscape. But the animals know more than we do."

Grant Jones

VOICES OF GRASS SHRUB TREE

A Story Like a Seed to Carry

In a packet, box,
Shimmers like a minnow,
You lure a tongue
To lick, crunch,
And be swallowed,
Carried for miles
To a dirt bed
Under trees where birds perch,
To be shat.
Or as letters with hooks
To be carried in our hair
Like gifts for your grandchildren.
Fragrant you tempt
Our gifts of pollen,
You baffle and dazzle us
To lick to life
Arouse, to die
For a kiss, deeper
To detour, until...
My beak becomes
A scribe for love,
A wetted quill
To write a poem.

Mouth of the Canyon of the Little Mosquito
Coyote Springs Farm
June 18, 2016

Spitting Out the Sand

After yesterday's swirling gale of dust
We're renewed to a pure blue calm--
Slicing the onions off the rockery wall
Boiling the tomatoes from under the veranda porch
Crushing the Serrano peppers with the heel of a knife
Brings the fragrant breaths of fall to Coyote Springs.

Coyote Springs Farm
Mouth of the Canyon of the Little Mosquito
Okanogan River Sub Basin
October 11, 2015

"Revolutionaries are lifelong students. So get used to going where everything is out of control and learn to feel comfortable in places where nobody has the answers. In view of today's problems, you actually have no other choice."

Grant Jones

VOICES OF ROCKS SAND FALLING WATER

Sleeping on Rocks

We lie
here in the noonday sun,
a couple of shadows on the forehead of Heggie's Rock,
    asleep.
It's dry where we are;
wet skins of water beside us
    seep
off this granite dome, the rock itself
like last week's petrified storm still
    melts,
in drifts laid the day before yesterday
when it migrated past and
    pelted.
We grow together beside other islands,
other flowering communities that
    swell.
Each drift expresses itself generation after generation;
as part of the same tapestry, and it
    flowers
as we leave a few grains of love
on the granite bed we've chosen that now
    dissolve,
grains of love that make
their way into vernal pools to
    nourish
the five-petalled, white stars,
and crimson corollas and to
    ooze
rainbows to the clouds that bunch
up over us like our elders as they
    pass.

Written at Heggie's Rock off the Old Louisville Road in Appling
Columbia County in the Piedmont of Georgia
March 7, 2009.

Land Shapes a Shaman's Song

Sagebrush and bitterbrush, water birch and Saskatoon,
Give us our grip to stay put
And keep from sliding.

Dogwoods and chokecherries, currents and willows,
Give us our tendons to twine
Together not break.

The Quaking Aspen and the Smooth Red Sumac,
Give us our flashing smiles, passion
To show our colors.

Old Ponderosas on the cliffs and Tamaracks in the swales,
Give us steadiness to survive and
Stand up tall.

The Black Cottonwoods by the river pump floods to the sky,
Give clouds for our dreams,
Year after year.

The lakes in the Highlands store snow and rain,
Give us sweet springs to remake
Our hearts each year.

And the metamorphic granites with their spalling quartzes
Remind my dentist in Oliver to change
His drill when I come in.

The animals, of course the animals, are all smarter than us
And give me whatever humility I possess,
With their wisdom and grace.

When spring's all over the Mariposa Lilies give me a jolt into
summer.

Coyote Springs Farm   December 1, 2016

A Steelhead bursts out of Mosquito Creek
Grant APRIL 7, 2016

VOICES OF CREATURES THAT SWIM CRAWL SLITHER

Something Red

Mosquito Creek roars, my heartbeat jumps,
It surges it sweeps it spits it spews,
Tearing out roots that hold down the barn.

The boulders under the footbridge shift,
Like loose and hungry cannon balls.
The planks are bending. Creak! The bridge tilts.

Nails pull and the boards start fighting.
Moon's first quarter rips our reach apart.
I don't think I'll be going to the barn tonight.

Wait, something red, flashes in the turn,
Ribbons dancing pulled upstream,
Wiggling in the bends, they're a couple feet long.

On a mission to drop their eggs in the gravel,
Be squirted by clouds in bursts of song
Sung on these trails for years to come.

Coyote Springs Farm
Mouth of the Canyon of the Little Mosquito,
(South Distributary of Mosquito Creek Watershed)
Okanogan Sub-Basin
South end of O'Neil Road at US Highway 97
One mile north of Ellis-Forde
April 7, 2016

chief of our Hidden Herd Grant
June 2016

VOICES OF CREATURES THAT WALK LEAP

Bone Dreamer
in memory of Bob MacDill, cowboy poet

I lived among coyotes at the mouth of the canyon.
I still wear the young pup's collarbone I found in the creek.
I heard his kettling, falsetto yipping.
But it's his spirit to play in the stars I keep.

I used to be as quick as a ferret but now
I'm so still flickers buzzbomb my hair
When I lean on a fencepost and go
Poo, yip poo, yip poo,
Poodi hoo, di yip poo, di yip poo,
Poo, yip poo, yip poo,
Poodi hoo, di yip poo, di yip poo.

Coyote Springs
Mouth of the Canyon of the Little Mosquito
North Okanogan Valley
December 13, 2014

As Sociable and Loving as Handsome Wolves

We crossed the river after dawn
as a fresh breeze from the north
blew the oily scent of lambs
off Whitestone Mountain's hip.
Leaves from the poplars had backfilled
the fence where seven lambs waited through the night.

Trailrunner George and mate Patti
broke the ridge first with Rendezvous Donal
followed by Teacher Scott.
Ranchfather Tom stood still by a tall poplar.
Shaman Grant and Healer Chong trailed in behind.
We came to slaughter seven lambs,
as sociable and loving as handsome wolves.

Shadows of morning banded Whitestone's knuckles
as we closed in circling the lambs.
George rolled the first to the ground and made
his end-of-the-trail mortise while Patti held down
and gentled the lamb, leaving its last breaths
to the wind in our hair under the tall poplars.

Note: None of this could have happened without Ranchmother Linda's energizing breakfast and lunch for the pack.

Black's Bench
Whitestone Mountain-Horse Springs Coulee Watershed
Okanogan River Sub Basin
October 17, 2015

"Everything is reaching out to you. Every animal and plant, every place, is striving for fullness, reaching out to you to be its partner."
Grant Jones

Eagles in the Elm over the Tractor Barn   G. Jones

VOICES OF CREATURES THAT FLUTTER FLASH SOAR

Part of the Weave

I started feeling younger when
I took up residence in
the mouth of this canyon
I became less hurried here,
relaxed, quieter, more awake.

When I sat still and rotated my head
like I was cranking a director's chair,
tiny movements caught my attention
tugged at the tapestry that unfurled
before me, like when I waded
the Sauk and baby cutthroat
would dart behind the boulders
or rotating fins of big browns
fanned sand in eddies up the Flathead:
my skin tightened its weave.

Its like that now—a pair
of Red-shafted Northern Flickers flick
from one vertical face of crumbling gneiss
to the next as they belay
to peck off the ants,
or a ground squirrel dashes
between balsamroots
or sometimes it's just a patch
of leaves that flash in a swirl
of warm air or something else
I can't name like the shadows
that twitch in the bitterbrush.
The tapestry out there is mine.
I am part of its weave.

On Watch Over Us Hill"
Mouth of the Canyon of the Little Mosquito
Mosquito Creek-Okanogan River Watershed
Okanogan River Sub Basin
December 16, 2015

41

Grant 9·26·2017

VOICES OF THE BUILDERS OF SHEDS GREAT BARNS AND OLD HOTELS

The Backhoe Shed

It's been good for my soul
Working with Reed,
Talking to the birch tree
Measuring for its flexations with the rafters
Staking the batter boards
Picking through the old posts and boards
From our recycle stack behind the barn,
Setting the pier boxes
Shooting the grades
Tightening up the stringlines
And centering the roach clips.
Mixing the mud
Pouring and placing the postbrackets
And screeding them off;

Waiting while they set-up overnight
Then stripping the forms,
Hearing a few songs
From the Bitterroot commune
Frosty Creek melodies
Brought down to the Eel and back again
To the skylines of the Antwyne...
Hearing Reed's homestead stories.

Yesterday my neighbor Bob,
Up the canyon on Wizard's Flat,
Shoveled, screened and loaded
Four yards of Beaverhead shale
In his International dumptruck
Piling it off our driveway so I can spread it
With the Kubota front-end loader
Dressing out the floor of the backhoe shed
Edged now with five ancient four-by-four
We got from Phil at Havillah Shake

Wood yard and sawmill down 97
Toward the Janis Rapids
Saving my countless ass
In every mutation we've triggered
Like when the barn collapsed
Or the house needed mutating,
Like when the tractor shed flooded
And the creek washed the road out,
Or when we needed the Camp Kitchen
To have a tall, hovering Tapanco roof,
Wanted a woodshed for a four-cord winter,
A deerfence around the vegetables,
Or portal gates to the Riverbraids Garden,
Beams for a footbridge to harbor our *minari*
The water celery that coils in our kimchi
Or posts to tie the moon
And keep the coyotes yipping
For any number of reasons
That keep the Earth in one piece.

Coyote Springs at the Mouth of the Canyon of the Little Mosquito
Mosquito Creek-North Okanogan Sub Watershed
June 6, 2015

The Backhoe Shed   G. Jones

Getting a Tour through the Globe

She led me through the Globe Building
to show me what she'd accomplished since way back last
Spring, and she introduced me to a few
new tenants in refurbished bays
off First Avenue, you know nothing too formal,
with a casual remark here and there,
"This is Grant, my partner in the Globe Building,"
"Hi," I said quizzically, "What a beautiful space
you'll have when your up and running,"
"So glad to meet you, Marilyn;
you from around these parts?"

As Ilze guided us through more doors and hallways into the
big new kitchen in the basement,
I told her what a great job she'd done,
how the old floors looked so beautiful,
how the patches old and new, were a polished history for
future generations to make up their own stories.

Big Doug firs that stood on
this ground were the first trees for
Yesler's sawmill in 1853 and
David Maynard built his Mercantile Exchange out of the
boards from these trees, and this
is where Maynard became "Doc" when the store became a
hospital in 1863.

This is also where Chief Seattle posed
for his photograph in 1865
by Edward M. Sammis from New York State.
It's where his daughter Kikisoblu befriended
Catherine Maynard in her home and where Catherine
gave Kikisboblu the name Angeline.
They were friends until Angeline died
in 1896.

Doc Maynard's place became the town's
first library in 1875.
It is also where Seattle's largest hotel,
The Arlington, stood four stories high
until the Great Fire consumed everything
in 1889.

May 15, 1890,
when the first bricks were laid for the Globe Building, the city
had transformed. A hundred and
twenty "fire-proof" brick buildings were
going up in the "Burn District" doubling the
population to 40,000.

By early in 1891 this
great, four-story stone
and brick Globe Building was completed--
twenty-one inch thick walls in the basement
nineteen inch on the first
and sixteen inch second and third
and twelve inch thick on the fourth.

But I wondered if they could see the hammer
kisses in the colossal, vertical grain
beams of Doug Fir from Henry Yesler's
mill and whether they could smell the burnt linseed oil in the
tongue-and-groove floor decking?

H.C. Schmidt's Saloon
is no longer on the corner upstairs; and
the Migliavacca Wine Company that sold un- adulterated,
California wine in the
basement under the areaway is gone
but you can still smell it when it rains.

The wainscoting in the halls upstairs
is the original paneling that graced the
corridors of Mrs. L. E. Jones's
Globe Hotel, but all her furniture
from New York City is gone now
as well as all her pretty paintings.

The big front doors swing smooth
into the lobby where her brother E. B. Masterson managed a
hundred rooms each with its own sink and woodstove. The
chestnut, yardage counter from Harry Lobell's clothing store
is still upstairs in the reception of Jones & Jones Architects,
Landscape Architects and Planners, Ltd.

And I wondered if they'd see the grease stains
in the brick from farm machines and engines
sold by Mitchell, Lewis and Staver or
if they'd smell the salt in the mortar from the Fireboat
Snoqualmie's five-inch stream of
seawater that dowsed the huge fire
started at two pm on the second floor
that exploded in the freight-elevator shaft when a can
of asphaltum burst, or was it booze,
that Wednesday on May 8th in 1901?

Pioneer Square Historic District
Elliott Bay, Mouth of the Duwamish River (Green River)
Central Puget Sound
The Salish Sea
September 5, 2015

The Globe Building, original name Marshall Walker Building, was designed by William E. Boone for
Ebenezer Marshall and Cyrus Walker in 1890 on Piner's Point.
Restoration architects: Jones & Jones.
Present owners since 1979, Globe Partners LLC,
Grant Jones, FASLA and Ilze Jones FASLA, AIA.
A block from here across Occidental Park was the famous Duwamish Village of 8 longhouses each
about 60 feet by 120 feet, called in Lushootseed, Djicjila'letc (djee-djee-lah-letsh) "little crossing over
place," home to 200 people. "Dzee-dzee-Lah-letch" was the largest village on Elliott Bay and home of
Si'ahl, Chief Seattle, warrior, orator and head of both the Duwamish and Suquamish Tribes.

When The Old Well Croaked

Cough, choke, are the faucets broke?
The hoses jerked and spurt.
Chirp, chirp, the tree frogs burped.
Has the well gone dry and croaked?

Called Jane: "It's a Dan thing," she said.
"I witched her at two hundred," he said,
"In that finger of granite below Bob and Jane's."
"It's suckin' air and the pump can't quit."

The water hissed deep down in that hole
So Larry pulled the lid off
Then Celso fixed the joint that'd split
And I kicked back on the switch.

She hummed, went quiet, the pipes stayed tight.
The hoses no longer spurt.
When Tree frog jumped I caught it in a bucket
But Garter snake slipped into the deep.

"You always wanted to live in an animal sanctuary,"
Reed said, from the ridge-beam of the car barn.
Well, Chong will have water for the potato soup
And I'll get a shower tonight.

In order of appearance: Jane Thompson, artist sculptor-house builder; Dan O'Connell, dowser witcher—well driller; Bob Thompson, farmer teacher house-builder; Larry Duncun, irrigation pump mechanic; Celso Pacheco-Pascacio, orchardist-farm manager-mechanic; Columbia Spotted Frog, (Rana pretiosa); Common Garter Snake (Thamnophis sirtalis); Reed Engel, journeyman carpenter—singer songwriter; Chong-Hui Jones, farmer—healer.

Written at the William Peterson homestead well, Coyote Springs Farm
Mouth of the Canyon of the Little Mosquito
Mosquito-Okanogan Reach
Okanogan River Sub-Basin
September 16, 2016

HOUSE
5 OCT 2017

GRT

VOICES OF THOSE WHO ALREADY LEFT

Now That We Know Where Gravity Comes From
For Janis Grinbergs 1914-2008

All your branches that ramified to the light
Of thirty-four thousand expanding dawns,
Each branch a finger of the sun's fiery heart,
Are down now, all down, trembling in the morning air
That fills our lungs and wafts between us
Whispering answers to the questions you kept
Reminding us to ask, like: "We still don't know
How electricity works or how to find the electrons."

But here you are, all ninety-four years
Of your ancient trunk lying on the ground
Flat as the long shadows of St. Peter's roof
That you painted as a steeplejack before you married
The pretty girl from the beaches of Jurmala
Who's waiting for you now to join her in Earth's warm bed,
Whispering the answer to your question of all questions:
"We still don't know where gravity comes from."

While here we are, the trees still standing
Measuring our days rooted in the ground
Of those who fell before and left
A hole for us to fill,
Now that we know where gravity comes from.

Richmond Highlands
Recited at Pacific Lutheran Cemetery Graveside Gathering
5 May 2008

Surrounded

The force that lifts
these strikeridges shifts
the wind that curls down canyon
brushes my cheeks
as the braiding creek
holds clouds in a mirror
that pulls my vision
down like a lanyard
hauls the wheel back on course
for my hunter's eye
to scan the footprints in the creek
feel spirits of dead men and women
swirl in my hair,
weave me their whispers.
Surrounded by the force,
I'm a basket in their hands
collecting dreams.

Mouth of the Canyon of the Little Mosquito
North Okanogan-Mosquito Creek Reach
Okanogan Sub-Basin
October 9, 2016

A CHORUS THAT COMINGLES IN THE RISING AIR

Creek in the Sky

A darkening sky swings over
the canyon this afternoon,
as our tomato and hot chili soup
simmers like rusty tea in my teeth.
Quakies twitch around my head
every time a fat raindrop hits
one of their brassy green leaves,
I get wheeled around and tilt
to blink, see riffles pass,
but when five leaves get whacked in unison,
I shake like an old tambourine flashing with trout.
My hair is wetted down
Like a beaver swimming my creek in the sky.
Changes must be coming.

Coyote Springs Farm
Mouth of the Canyon of the Little Mosquito
Okanogan Sub Basin

Hello!

I will not be banished from here.
Mold made me and will have me again.
Clouds may lift me a mile or two
But I'll return back here again.
Nothing big but everything small,
I'll never leave this place,
It has me contained.
This is it.
Nothing new,
Everything old.
And here I am.

Hello!

Coyote Springs
25 August 2015

Song of the Windlovers

Oh, there they are, standing taller now
Day after day when we come down canyon
Mornings after breakfast. Look how they shun
Those sleek Foxjaw Kenworths, filled with harvest apples
And those Winnebagos dragging yesterday to tomorrow.

> *Oh, there they are, standing taller,*
> *Day after day, when we come down canyon.*

At five stories high, they pull up coolness
From the looping meanders of the Okanogan
"Rendezvous" they named it, the Old Chiefs,
This path of their moccasins for ten thousand years
It glides down south, under the cottonwoods
Across the tracks, heading for Oregon
Down the gorge and over the bar.

> *At five stories high, they pull up the coolness*
> *From the looping meanders of the Okanogan.*

Afternoons, after wind's up,
When we come down canyon for the mail, they wave "Hello,"
They sway like arms, and flutter like fingers,
Their crowns shivering to the puffs off the hills,
Make their leaves spin, thousands flash
Their eyes that blink riffles between gusts.

> *In the afternoons, after wind's up,*
> *When we come down canyon for the mail, they wave "Hello."*

Listen to them whisper, sing in rounds,
Hum like waterfalls that pump straight to the clouds.
As the gale freshens, they hunch and shudder,
Shaking out wind, branches whirling,
Suddenly they're dancers, with kicking skirts flying,
Their limbs reach for the sky, vibrate and coil

To the gusts that strum them, like zithers or kayágums.

Listen to them whisper, sing in rounds,
And hum like waterfalls that pump straight to the clouds.

There's a storm today, our "windlovers" are horses.
They bolt from the gates, bent at the shoulders,
They bow all together and pulse in waves.
When they roar to full pitch, a low-middle octave,
Turn to love the sweet wind's power,
They calm themselves, careening as a group,
Huddle like a fleet of pirates luffing
Behind the bar, swigging their rum,
As our Staghorn Sumacs, break in two.

Oh, there they are they're taller now
Day after day, when we come down canyon.
At five stories high, they pull up coolness
From the looping meanders of the Okanogan.
In the afternoons, after wind's up
When we come down canyon for the mail,
They wave a "Hello."
Listen to them whisper, sing in rounds,
They hum like waterfalls, pumping straight to the clouds.

With the Lombardy Poplars bordering Jones Nursery Gardens
Along the south end of O'Neil Road and up the driveway to Coyote
Springs Farm in the Mouth of the Canyon of the Little Mosquito
(The South Distributary Reach of Mosquito Creek)
Okanogan River Sub-Basin
July 31, 2016

A FAMILY OF CLOUDS TO WATCH OVER US

Who's to Say Whose Eyes Are Better

Something different woke the coyotes up canyon last night,
Seemed to tighten their throats to a humming moan.
Then lightning shuddered, thunder rocked
And the aspens, who watch through our predawn window,
Splattered the ceiling with their tribulations
Like heart-shaped shadows in hues of blue neon.

It's been way too long since we last talked
You and I, and I need to finish
This poem that's kept me awake for two weeks now.
Yes it's another poem about *Populus tremuloides,*
The Quaking Aspens that Chong planted to heal me.

If I can tell you a little more about what they're capable of,
Share my feelings of awe with you, if that's possible,
Perhaps a story about their welcoming nature,
Then maybe they'll live in your heart the day after tomorrow.

So it was that later this morning
We bushwacked up the canyon past the waterfall
To visit the spring we named after our coyotes.
We've had some hot spells over a hundred degrees
But the creek's always cold, at fifty-two.
Wading, eyes open for little Steelhead fry
Wiggling in the eddies, and
There they were!

It was later the aspens made sign as we stopped
To sigh before sliding into their sprouting shade.
A grove like this is a single individual,
Probably a male if high up the mountain ridge,
But probably a female down here in the valley,
Its thousands of leaves had seen us coming

Long before we got there to rest from the heat,
Where we each leaned against fresh copies of itself

Those identical white trunks called ramets by our scientists.

We heard gurgles from the spring, above the bank,
There where moose prints crossed in the mud.
We realized now, their leaves had stopped trembling.

Who's to say whose eyes are better,
Which of our skins feels pleasure first,
Whose bones first heard that thunder rumble
Before the fire ignites, where it cleans and feeds
The seeds of flowers that will smile next spring
Where trails of firedance ran, where each birthing
Began and renewed the land, breathing?

Mouth of the Canyon of the Little Mosquito
Mosquito Creek Reach of the North Okanogan
Okanogan River Sub-Basin
July 21, 2016

A Few Thoughts on My Birthday

I've been this way all my life;
I listened to rivers, learned to sing.
Sat with ancient cedars in the rain
Watched raindrops be rivulets in fissures of bark
Transposed, transfigured, transmigrated,
Transmutated and
Became a river.
It isn't easy to be a river.
Even though trees talk to you, widen your span;
And you whisper back under their arches.
People can't hear you,
But birds seem to know.
Rocks breathe.
Peaks and mesas undress.
Talus bloom butterflies. Pikas whistle.
Mountains watch for signs of respect
Cry when ignored, even moan.
So I share what I know
With those who fly, swim, crawl and walk,
Sway, shimmer, sough and quake.

Because those who talk out loud
Have lost ears for this kind of music.
I'm a shaman and I write poems
As a way to converse without ridicule,
To share what I see and what I hear.
The land gives me my inner voice,
Feels the weight of me on the ledges.
And the river covers my tracks in the sand.

Coyote Springs Farm
Mouth of the Canyon of the Little Mosquito
August 29, 2015

Looking North   G Jones

STORIES IN MORNING MIST AND AFTERNOON RAIN

Letter to Mike

So glad you're still casting
your well timed words as arcs of light;
these magic currents of time
slip between our fingers like the Sandhill Cranes
above the Okanogan River at this moment sailing south to
Mexico for the winter, singing and jabbering to themselves
while I lie on my cot under my camp kitchen roof
lobbing words to you another fisherman.

Coyote Springs Farm
September 17, 2013

Retiring

Retiring for me, was a form of pioneering
Learning how to slip out, the haunted
City's door,
Leave the tideflats,
The pains in the stricken and dying estuary,
To explore the Great Columbian Plain,
Looking for some tributary, lobe of prairie and highland
Clean from centrifugal,
Backspinning chatter
To find a watershed, with which to partner,
To restore the ground, and plant trees not for money,
But to make fresh oxygen and flowers
To pollinate Earth-Mother,
Pump up her whole organismal resuscitation.
I wanted to discover, I mean honor and love,
A landscape on my own terms, with my own feelings,
And a community too
If I felt like it and had the time.

I wanted to watch clouds form overhead, like my thoughts,
To get forgotten, before I'm gone, when I can still
Enjoy it, since nobody else seems to care.
Retiring was a primal opportunity to fall off my horse
And hit, the ground, where it smells good,
Or crash like a steelhead in a creek nobody hears,
Where the coyotes and my shepherds "Luna" and "Wolfie"
Bark at the moon.

Coyote Springs Farm
May 14, 2016

Questions on Healing

This morning's mingling fingers
advancing air of fall entangle the
Saskatoon and dogwood, and their tendons
breathe scents that tingle my nostril hairs
as I follow Chong's sinewy, brown legs
up braids through the creek, behind the barn.

Then those cool fingers tap me on the shoulder and ask:
What the hell would you be doing if you'd stayed in the city?

Would I still be alive or dead and gone?
Well, the springs that feed this creek,
watering shrubs long quivered for arrows,
they healed my blood and sutured my nerve lines.
They'll connect me with the life force here, many falls to come,
following those brown and sinewy legs
up the braids in the creek behind the barn

Where those cool fingers tap you on the shoulder and ask:
Any more questions?

Coyote Springs Farm
Mouth of the Canyon of the Little Mosquito
Okanogan Sub-Basin
August 12, 2017

Coyote Springs, Peterson Homestead, Little Mosquito Creek below
Beaverhead, Pickens Range

VOICES THAT PRY OPEN AND SET US STRAIGHT

Falling in Love with the Land Is Not Easy to Explain

I guess it was the creek that captured me first.
I fell in love with the sky second,
then the rock outcrops and escarpments,
then trails and scattered trees.

Down in the valley where we are, no forest exists--
gallery ribbons of red-twigged dogwood,
river birch and a few huge cottonwoods.
Skeins of aspen stems tremble and quake,
underground rootlets spring out of the ground
around seeps that perch
along the benches of the hill slopes, but otherwise
it's all bunchgrass and sagebrushes
and bitterbrush, sometimes we call greasewood.

The greasewood is blooming now with creamy flowers.
It's a harsh community with ticks and rattlers
so it's not so easy to fall in love with.
There's sadness too in our dying
Ponderosas who've survived so long
so long careening out from cracks in cliffs.
But now in rising heat and desiccation
they're succumbing to bark beetles.
Slowly turn brassy green before collapsing.

It's more like this landscape survives and doesn't complain,
causing you to take stock of your own precious
fragile and tough body, love it more and respect it
for its own persistence and scrappy survival.
Of course it's made us love our marriage partnership as well.
We became pioneers who will be buried here,
a pair who've rooted in and made a home.

It's kind of scary sometimes;
but it's also the way it is, the way things have to be.
So we decided to love it for its self, ugly or not,
beautiful or not, common, singularly unique body.

It's very complicated and simple simultaneously.
Small chunks of hornblende granite spall
off our cheeks into the lips of the coulee after dark.
I hope I'm making sense.

Coyote Springs Farm
Mouth of the Canyon of the Little Mosquito
30 April 2015

In Something Other than Prose

For my friends who write poetry

My mind's mine, all mine.
For me, to write poems, is scholarly research;
I make raw discoveries every time.

What I find in the tunnels, streams and caves of my brain
Refreshes me, leads me on like a coyote.
I write for myself to keep a record of
The holes I fall into and vistas that open.
Each poem's a view up my tributaries,
Eyes into my wellsprings, to share.

I appreciate your poems you share with me
And those you send, from you other shaman friends,
Because each poem is perfect and real, alive and
Looking through its own eyes, like a deer or a trout,
Tremulous but steady, it breathes in like a fern,
Like a pine on the ledges, or a sequoia that makes circles.

Writing in prose, it saps my strength.
Why would I convince others of something I already know?
Prove it for what? What a waste of time.
Getting an "A" doesn't give us our identity.
So I will always write, in something other than prose.

Coyote Springs Farm
At the mouth of the Canyon of the Little Mosquito
Mosquito Creek Watershed
Okanogan River Sub-Basin

our Great Gray 2011·2013 GRJ

AND WHACK US ABOUT THE HEAD WHEN WE'RE NOT LISTENING

The Animals Are Talking

Walk past the barn to the spillway,
Where Bobcat crossed the creek last night.
Her tracks curve through the aspen glade,
Skirting past the homestead iron pile,
They veer on up the dugroad grade
That we restored to the pocket-bench
On the shoulder of Pack Pony Hill
Where we carried the loveseat and two chairs
To watch sunsets that shimmer up the river bend.
That was last summer before talking heads
Began lying like scheming magpies on the fence.
Bobcat's prints were close spaced
As she walked out there, slow in the moonlight,
Drove "Wolfie" crazy to growl and bark,
To guard the house where we slept
On our hot-granite slab by the fire
Under a hand-tied comforter.
She was tracking a snowshoe rabbit
Who foraged on Saskatoon buds,
Fir needles, and stems of Sagebrush buttercups,
Under the long December Cold Moon.
America was shuddering in its longest night.
Here, follow my tractor tracks
Behind the house up the Pine Trail Road
Where mulleins lay like shadows under the snow
Felled by Chong-hui's razor sickle,
Next to the clumps of yarrows and lupines
Where bluebells and spring beauties poke
Like antennae through the snow waiting.

Coyote came down off Watch-Over-Us Hill,
Stood where you're standing, thinking to himself:
    "Everything is connected, though most of you
    Seem only tied to each other,
    And fewer and fewer of you to Earth."

Mouth of the Canyon of the Mosquito at Ellis-Forde 12/24/2016

Sauntering

John Muir on Hiking – "I don't like either the word or the thing. People ought to saunter in the mountains – not hike! Do you know the origin of that word 'saunter'? It's a beautiful word. Away back in the Middle Ages people used to go on pilgrimages to the Holy Land, and when people in the villages through which they passed asked where they were going, they would reply, 'A la sainte terre', 'To the Holy Land'. And so they became known as sainte-terre-ers or sauterers. Now these mountains are our Holy Land, and we ought to saunter through them reverently, not 'hike' through them."

It's still so cold. Nothing
blooming yet. The minari water celery
in the creek has no white blooms
to collect and take with other flowers
to the cemetery. I have always lagged behind,
following scents. I stop frequently
to listen to the tongues
fluttering in the trees.
Sometimes on the trail I feel cold spots
and hairs on my neck shiver me.
That's when I can thank
The spirits who linger there.

Mars Day
March 27, 2018
Coyote Springs Farm

84

You Remember

Ah, yes, the rungs of the ladder,
the passion and dying,
heavenly flesh flaking,
spores spalling,
the frog leaping
from the hot pan
into the stunning cold
under the boulders of the creek.
You remember.

Back then, you had the juice and blood
to climb high up the fir tree, smelling
the lemon balmy needles, sucking
the sap off your fingers.
Yes, I rested at every whorl
up the trunk, feeling the slight tremors
between my thighs
before the swaying began.
You remember.

Each tree you climbed too, felt you,
offered its handholds to the sky.
Each tree was a little different from the last;
each taught you with those sways it made,
when to stop, when to hug,
get peaceful, and clear-eyed
like an eagle at sunset.
They made you strong.
You remember.

Now,
sitting on this rock above the canyon,
beginnings and endings
are one, as I exhale and breathe,
my braiding creek has straightened out
between the cottonwoods above the barn,
retracted for the summer just

like my tendons slide by inside
their own fascia in my leg
as I take a rest after climbing up here.
You remember

how snow bulged behind the spillway
four times between dawns
to the pullings of the moon,
just as sandbars came and went
in coves of the Salish Sea--
to this ebb, flood, ebb, flood
each day, pulsing quietly until it broke,
gushing ice over the dam like tidewater
pouring at midnight over the lips of the dropoff.
You remember.

Then, one day you wake up in the tall
grass where your grandad is scything,
and there you are, wobbling
beside your Collie dog,
reliving those old passions,
those sparking moments stored
behind your eyes in your cave of treasures
as you race with me to the end of the line
nobody will remember.

Written somewhere between Waimanalo, Wanapum, Wellfleet, Wasilla,
and Wooloomooloo

Consciousness Rises in the Arroyo

After midnight I cracked open one eye
and three stars blinked
above Beaverhead.

At dawn a light snow began to fall
and a silvery old fencepost fell down
in a wind gust.

That fencepost now is draped all white,
the cosmic-powder heaping
like a grave.

But my consciousness rises in the arroyo
behind the house, down deep
in the compost.

Young passions are building,
and mine still beautiful,
but to old to act on.

Coyote Springs Farm
Valentine's Day
February 14, 2018

The Voices of Coyote Springs Farm

These voices of grass, shrub and tree,

of rock, sand
and falling water,
these voices of creatures
that ooze and swim,
crawl, slither,
walk, leap,
flutter, flash and
soar, and raise
a chorus from the mouth
of the canyon that commingles
in rising air, and
makes families of clouds
gather to watch over us,
they whisper our stories
by morning mist,
by smiling swirls
of afternoon rain,
to set us straight,
pry us open
to where we're heading,

then whack us about the head

when we're talking not listening
to the transcendent symphony
of voices singing.

Coyote Springs Farm
May 24, 2016

Grant Taking in the View from Beaverhead   W Henze

Landscapes need human stewards to reciprocate with them to increase their energy and long-lastingness at every scale.

Grant Jones

Grant Jones was born August 29, 1938 on a small saltwater farm at Richmond Beach in the northern reaches of the Central Puget Sound Region of the Salish Sea Estuary, to a Welsh-Irish Canadian father and a Quaker English/Irish-American mother. He began writing poetry at the age of eleven, but found his unique voice as one of Theodore Roethke's poets in the fabled Advanced Verse writing class that Roethke conducted from 1961 to 1964 when he was Poet in Residence at the University of Washington. Jones is Founding Principal of Jones & Jones Architects, Landscape Architects and Planners, Ltd., with Ilze Jones in 1969 and Johnpaul Jones in 1972, maintaining an international design practice in the historic Globe Building in Pioneer Square over the last forty-five years. Since 2006 he has made his home in the North Okanogan Valley in North Central Washington, where he and his wife Chong-hui have created the Jones Gardens at Coyote Springs Farm at the mouth of the canyon of the Little Mosquito between Tonasket and Oroville.

His landscape poetry is recognized as a fundamental part of his intrinsic design approach and integral to his research and scholarship in landscape architecture, ecological design and landscape conservation planning. He is an Affiliate Professor in the Department of Landscape Architecture at the College of Built Environment of the University of Washington in Seattle, and has held teaching positions at Harvard, the University of Oregon, UC Berkeley, University of Virginia and Texas A&M, and has lectured at over thirty-five universities on ecological design, landscape planning and poetry. He is the recipient of over thirty design awards including the Richard Neutra Medal, the President's Award for Excellence and the first Firm of the Year Award bestowed by the ASLA. He is a Frederick Sheldon Fellow of Harvard University and a Glimcher Fellow of the Knowland School of Architecture at The Ohio State University. He was inducted to the Roll of Honor at the College of Built Environments at the University of Washington in April of 2015. He is the first recipient of the LAF Medal from the Landscape Architecture Foundation's 50th Anniversary in June of 2016 in recognition of his vision and leadership as Director of Education and for launching the Olmsted Scholarships.

Several poems in this collection have been published in: *What Rocks Know selected poems of Grant Jones; Okanogan Poems Volume 1, Okanogan Poems Volume 2* seventeen poets, Skookumchuck Press, as well as in *Okanogan Poems Volume 3 landscapes are observatories, The Skookumchuck Poems,* and *In Love With Your Place,* published through the CreateSpace publishing house of Amazon Books and available for purchase and shipping directly from Amazon. Some of the poems have also been published in *The Fullness,* Landscape Journal; *Seeing, Where Logic and Feelings Meet,* Landscape Architecture Magazine; *Grant Jones: A Plan for Puget Sound,* Princeton Architectural Press Sourcebook 4 by Jane Amidon; and *The Methow Naturalist.*; and in *Naming Water 48 Poems by Grant Jones and Mike Robinson, Skookumchuck Press. Listening to the Voice of the Earth,* an autobiographical journal of stories, sketches and poems with educational lessons and design guidelines will be published by the author in 2019.

"Every landscape has its code, and if you fall in love with it and give it a voice, the poems you unearth from it will forever give you a place to stand as partner and friend and lover."

Grant Jones

AFTERWORD

Jones Riverbraids Arboretum Story

Coyote Springs Farm
Landscape Restoration History
Grant Jones, Spring 2013

We started up with a lot of tiny plants close together in the nursery (30x70ft) next to the farmhouse back in 2007 and from them we slowly created the Riverbraids Arboretum out in the field along O'Neil Road to the west. Instead of making a rectangular fenced nursery in the 15-acre field down there, we decided to make a hundred "islands with rings," each planted with a single species. In other words some islands are trees, some shrubs, 10 to 30 individuals in each. All together I think we planted about 2,000 plants in separate holes in the grass.

With the Massey-Ferguson M35 diesel, I mow the curvilinear paths between the islands and around their rings, as well as the wider grass paths around the perimeters of the arboretum. It's sort of like a string of atolls with braided grass channels weaving between them with grassy service paths around the borders of the property. Mowing the grass, sickling around each plant as well as widening the holes around each one helps to keep them growing without being suffocated by the grasses. I mow inside the circles and around the interior islands with an old Jacobsen Turfcat. It's hydrostatic and spins on a dime making it easy to use in the tight quarters of the interior island circles. More about this later.

The first year we covered about 40 percent of the 15-acre field, actually the southwest quadrant and half the southeast. The second year we planted out the northwest and the northeast quadrants. Each island is sort of a miniature nursery, an idea Rob Crandall of Methow Natives Nursery in Winthrop proposed during a visit to help us when we were getting started. As the plants mature and grow together tighter, we can thin out a few of them and plant those in separate new islands, or sell them, or give them away to friends.

Basically we are restored the old abandoned Floyd Thornton apple orchard to an island braidwork of plant communities, mostly native conifers and broadleaf trees, native deciduous shrubs, and farmstead traditional plants. The northwest has mostly hardy nuts/acorns along with Giant Sequoia and White Cedar. The northeast, is mostly native and other hardy forest buffer plants. O'Neil Road along the west and the orchard road on the south are edged by an outer perimeter of Lombardy poplars flanked behind by Ponderosa pines and Douglas firs to block the views from the outside and to give the "islands" inside a little more privacy. So that's the general concept fo Riverbraids Arnoretum Nursery.

The sandy hill slope on the east is unirrigated and traversed by several mown trails which are more like half-bare sandy dirt so eventually they will get some dry-site native seed mix from Methow Natives in Winthrop in the upper Methow Valley.

Across the brow of this sideslope along the eastern perimeter there's a tunnel of Siberian elm (Ulmus pumila) and Black locust (Robinia psuedoacacia) that has an old tractor path inside it. Right above that and parallel with it there's another tractor path which skirts the west lip of the old canal-flume ditch that lies dry now, slowly filling up with Siberian elm (which we intend to fell), flanked with Sage (Artemisia) with a few Ponderosa pine. Above that there's a sagebrush covered sandy bench (aeolian loess blown in off the top of the Ancient Soyoos Glacier ten-thousand years ago); and this bench tilts and steepens to form a low hill punctured and crested with several cockscomb outcrops of metamorphic Hornblende Gneiss that stretch along the contours northward like small rimrock ramparts.

Bob Kennedy helped us backhoe-in a narrow road with our Kubota L-35 diesel front-end loader tractor and I back-bladed it out with my Massey-Ferguson M-35 diesel farm tractor's three-point blade. The road begins down at the field barn in the arboretum and snakes up the sideslope past the old concrete cistern at the south end of the abandoned canal ditch. The road path then doglegs northeast and then turns back southeast until it gets you up over the bench where we put up the teepee camp each spring and then it traverses southwestward back down through a little coulee that spills off Watch Over Us Hill, curling right into the backyard under the Planetrees next to our farm house, thus connecting the Riverbraids Arboretum in the old Stansbury Homestead field to our Coyote Springs oasis (the old William Peterson Homestead in Little Mosquito Creek Canyon. The new road path is in pure loess sand. Bob Thompson (Wizardworks), our neighbor who lives with his wife Jane up the canyon, hauled down his red shale gravel off Beaverhead Mountain which rises straight up behind their place with his International Harvester diesel dumptruck and spread it the length of this snaking hairpin-bended trail. No other contractor but Bob would have tackled this mission or would have possessed the skill to pull it off. Chong hand-broadcast seeded the roadpath with five native grasses and wildflowers from Methow Natives: Idaho fescue (Festuca idahoensis), Sand dropseed (Sporobolus cryptandrus), Bluebunch wheatgrass (Agropyron spicatum), Yarrow (Achillea millefolium), and Snow buckwheat Eriogonum viveum). Roger Rylander transplanted Ponderosa pines from the nursery next to the house (2-3 feet tall) on both sides of the road path and irrigated them with continuous stretches of black PVC ¾ inch pipe coil with drip emitters at each pine hole, plus continuous 1 inch black PVC pipe coil with sprinklers to cover the seed spread over the half-sand-half shale gravel road. We call this curvaceous beauty of a roadpath the "Pine Trail."

It was back in September of 2012 on Craigslist we found the big diesel Turfcat II DW220 with 21.5 HP and hydrostatic steering made by Kubota for Jacobsen. It was on a wheat farm south of Milton-Freewater, Oregon near a small town called Athena. We decided to drive through there on our way from Seattle to Oroville. Kind of a long jaunt but we wanted to see the country and to meet pioneer wheat farmers Richard King and his wife, Celine, both in the 80s. The King's showed us around the many huge straw fields they cut with their combines right after the peas are harvested, across thousands of acres. It was fun touring their territory and they were so impressed that we took the time to come down to see them that they decided to haul the mower up to Oroville two days later (a six hour drive). We paid for their gas. This big old machine is 3-wheeled with the engine in the back, the seat in the middle and the mowing deck in front with two rotary blades. This park-golf-course mower is perfect for doing the ring paths inside the islands and it can turn on a dime.

Chong sickles the grass out around each tree and shrub and from around the solid-set irrigation uprights that carry the sprinklers, using a traditional Korean sickle with a gently curving, razor sharp 12 inch blade. I sharpen them each morning. I mow and mow and mow, day after day, using the Massey-Ferguson tractor with an old 6-foot John Deere mower-deck on the main paths and the Jacobsen Kubota Turfcat park mower inside each island's moon ring.

The Riverbraids Arboretum Plant List, sixty-eight different species so far:

Abies koreana—Korean Fir
Acer glabrum douglasii—Douglas Maple
Acer grandidentatum—Canyon Maple
Acer negundo—Box Elder Maple
Acer platanoides—Norway Maple
Acer rubrum—Red Maple
Amelanchier alnifolia—Saskatoon Serviceberry
Betula occidentalis —Western Water Birch
Betula platyphylla japonica—Jap. White Birch
Betula lenta—Sweet Yelow Birch
Caragana arborescens –Siberian Pea shrub
Chaenomeles japonica—Japanese Quince
Chamaecyparis lawsoniana—Lawson Falsecypress
Cornus mas—Korean Cornelian Cherry Dogwood
Cornus stolonifera—Red-twigged Dogwood
Crataegus douglasii—Douglas Hawthorn
Diospyros species—Korean Persimmon
Elaeagnus angustifolia—Russian Olive
Fraxinus pennsylvanica—Green Ash
Gingko biloba—Maidenhair Tree

Gleditsia triacanthos—Thorny Honeylocust
Juniperus scopulorum—Rocky Mt. Juniper
Juglans cinerea—Butternut
Juglans nigra—Eastern Black Walnut
Juglans regia carpathian—Carpathian Walnut
Kolkwitzia amabilis--Beauty Bush
Larix occidentalis—Western Larch
Magnolia soulangeana—Saucer Magnolia
Malus fuji—Fuji Apple
Metasequoia glyptostroboides—Dawn Redwood
Morus alba—White Mulberry
Platanus acerifolia—London Plane Tree
Phellodendron amurense—Amur Cork Tree
Philadelphus lewisii—Lewis' Mock Orange
Picea glauca—White Spruce
Pinus ponderosa—Ponderosa Pine
Populus nigra italica—Lombardy Poplar
Populus tremuloides—Quaking Aspen
Populus trichocarpa—Black Cottonwood
Pseudotsuga menziesii glauca—Blue Douglas Fir
Prunus armeniaca--Apricot
Prunus maackii—Amur Chokecherry
Prunus serotina—Black Cherry
Prunus virginiana--Choke Cherry
Pyrus malus—Cultivated Apple
Quercus alba—Eastern White Oak
Quercus macrocarpa—Bur Oak
Rhus glabra—Western Smooth Sumac
Rhus typhina—Staghorn Sumac
Ribes aureum—Golden Currant
Ribes sanguineum—Winter Red Current
Robinia pseudoacacia—Black Locust
Salix alba vitellina—Vitelli Golden Willow
Salix bebbiana—Bebb Willow
Salix babylonica—Weeping Willow
Salix exigua—Coyote Willow
Salix matsudana Aztec—Globe Willow
Sambucus cerulea—Blue Elderberry
Shepherdia argentea—Silver Buffaloberry
Sorbus americana—American Mountainash
Symphoricarpus albus—Common Snowberry
Sequoia gigantea—Sequoia Big Tree
Thuja occidentalis—American Eastern White Arborvitae
Thuja plicata—American Western Red Arborvitae
Ulmus pumila—Siberian Elm
Viburnum dentatum—Arrowwood

Viburnum trilobum—American Cranberry Bush
Vitis labrusca and vinifera (inter-specific cross Arkansas 1258 x
Arkansas Muscat==" Neptune," "Jupiter,' and "Reliance" seedless grapes

Future Plants under consideration are:

Acer ginnala "Bergiana Flame"—Amur Maple super red
Acer saccharinum—Silver Maple
Actinidia arguta—Kiwi Goosebery
Actinidia kolomitka—Russian Gooseberry
Amelanchier Canadensis—Shadblow Serviceberry
Aronia melanocarpa—Black Chokecherry
Betula populifolia—Gray Birch
Carpinus betulus—European Hornbeam
Catalpa bignonioides—American Catalpa
Cercis Canadensis—American Eastern Redbud
Cornus alternifolia—Pagoda Dogwood
Corylus cornuta—Beaked Hazelnut
Elaeagnus communtata—Silverberry
Forsythia "Meadowlark"—Meadowlark Forsythia
Fraxinus Americana—American Ash
Hamemelis virginiana—Common American Witch Hazel
Juglans nigra—Black Walnut
Maackia amurensis—Amur Maackia
Physocarpus capitatus—Pacific Ninebark
Populus x Canadensis "Prairie Sky"—Prairie Sky Poplar
Quercus palustris--Pin Oak
Populus alba richardii--Richard's Poplar
Sorbus alnifolia—Korean Mountainash
Sorbus aucuparia—European Mountainash
Ulmus pumila—Siberian Elm
Vitis riparia—Riverbank Grape

Our neighbor, Celso Pacheco, is now our farm manager and I am finally relieved of
the mowing and irrigating.

Grant and Chong

www.ingramcontent.com/pod-product-compliance
Lightning Source LLC
Chambersburg PA
CBHW081140090426

42736CB00018B/3419